AF250297

Part Of My Life in

Poem

Judith Juste

Part Of My Life in Poem
Copyright © 2021 by Judith Juste

I would love to thank everyone who contributed to the making and
publication of my book.

Photo credit: Andrew MacLeod from Gecko Foto
Makeup: Bisma Studio and Meredith Juste
Hair: Judith Juste
Eyebrows: Merle Norman Cosmetic Studio
Eyelashes: Douha Dahdouh

All rights reserved. No part of this publication may be reproduced,
distributed, or transmitted in any form or by any means, including
photocopying, recording, or other electronic or mechanical
methods, without the prior written permission of the author, except
in the case of brief quotations embodied in critical reviews and
certain other non-commercial uses permitted by copyright law.

Tellwell Talent
www.tellwell.ca

ISBN
978-0-2288-5634-4 (Paperback)
978-0-2288-5635-1 (eBook)

Dedication

This collection of poems is an autobiography. It talks about me, my life, my sorrows, my joys, my sufferings, my loves; it's about me. One day, on the verge of suicide, I thought life wasn't worth living, that my life was not worth living. I didn't feel loved by anyone. I felt like a stranger whether I was in my own country or next to my own mother. I would like to tell all the people who are going through hard times or who are feeling abandoned that the light is at the end of the tunnel. I dedicate my poems to all the women who have lived humiliation, who have been mistreated and abused whether by their partner or their family, or who have been rejected by society. Do not be discouraged. I dedicate my book to all the single women out there who, abandoned by their partner, are forced to work hard every day to take care of their children. I dedicate my book to all parents who are doing their best to ensure that their children have the best life possible. I dedicate my book to all people who think that life is meaningless. I wish for you to find peace, and I hope these poems find you in the moment you need it the most.

About me / Introduction

I was born in the Republic of Haïti in a village called Camp-Perrin located in the southern department. Les Cayes is the capital. I am from a country and a family that had nothing to offer me other than misery and sadness. My grandmother Mila was donated by my great-grandmother Idamé as a servant to a rich family in the village. Mila took care of their children. In return, the family was supposed to feed her, because my great-grandmother couldn't afford to feed her. My grandmother was nineteen when she became pregnant after being raped by the family's son. Thrown out in the streets by the family, she was forced to return to her mother. When my mother was born, her alleged father sent an old maid to check if the child was really his daughter even though he knew perfectly well that he had raped my grandmother and that the child was his own. Yet the old maid told him that the child was too white to be his, and he believed her because he was black and so was my grandmother. However, he had forgotten that his father had white skin and so did my mother's great-grandmother. Mixing often creates different skin colours over generations. Because of this skin colour story, he abandoned my mother. My grandmother and my great-grandmother were left in the deepest misery. Despite everything, he got married to a woman of French descent and had two other children who looked nothing like him. My mother, on the other hand, was the perfect portrait of her father.

Although my mother was one of the smartest kids in her school, and her father had the capacity to help her, he didn't do anything to help her in any way. Because she had no one to finance her studies, she couldn't reach her full potential. My mother told me that twice a day she passed by her grandparents' house to go to school while her grandfather sat in the front patio. Not once did he ask her if she was hungry or needed anything.

Before going to Les Cayes for her exams, my mother went to ask her father for help to buy a pair of shoes. He answered her, "Gertrude, do you know if I have any money saved for this?" My mother felt humiliated. Another time, when my mother needed help to go to the nursing school in Cap-Haïtien, my mom went with her grandmother to ask for help from her father again. Her father, who was the judge at the court De Cassation of Cayes, answered my mom's grandmother that she could enrol my mom in the nursing school by herself. He knew very well that she needed someone in a higher position to refer her to that particular school; otherwise, she would have no chance of getting accepted into the nursing school. Also, my mom's grandma didn't have the money to send her to the nursing school. Desperate, my mother went to ask the Catholic sisters of the Camp-Perrin school for help to get into the nursing school, but they told her that she was too small to be a nurse because she would not be able to see the patients on the operating table. Only her father's intervention would have allowed her to enter the nursing school if he was willing to help her and pay for her education. The Catholic sisters of Camp-Perrin offered her a position of professor at the school. She didn't have any other choice but accept this offer at the same school where she had studied with the same sisters who hadn't helped her to get into the nursing school. After all, my mother was only the daughter of the maid of her father's family.

According to my birth certificate, my father was a peasant and my mother was a teacher. I started to write at a young age. From what I can remember, when I was maybe nine years old, my mother was not interested in what I was writing. I think she didn't know that I was writing. I published my first collection of poetry at the age of twenty, encouraged by my cousin Marie Laurette who was a journalist. She got me an interview for my book with her journalist friend on national television. Soon after, I travelled to Montréal where I started writing again without thinking about publishing my poems. When I got to Montréal, I didn't have any connections or the money to publish. I kept my little booklet everywhere with me. Thirty years have passed since then. Now that my life is more stable, I want my readers to know me, to know what I went through in my life.

I didn't know my father well. The first time I saw my father I was nine years old and the second time I was maybe about sixteen years old. My mom never spoke to me about him. At the age of thirteen, though I was innocent, my mother allowed her boyfriend Robertson to whip me copiously with a leather rope made with braided dried goatskin. Why? Because I had received a love letter from a young boy named Loulou who was living in the area. Meanwhile, my mother had no time for my sister and me. She taught school every day. Besides, she had to take care of her man. Every day, he left 50 Haitian gourdes on the night table so that my mother could cook him his preferred food of "bouillon". After she served him, she watered the rest down to feed us. After all this, her man didn't have any respect for her. He was running after all the women in the neighbourhood. Sadly, this man had nothing to offer her. On top of all of that, she had to go sell her cookies and candies at the flea market.

All my life, I was constantly inhabited by the thought that I was worthless and that my presence on Earth was completely futile. I was convinced that I had no reason to be in this world; I did not matter to anyone. In this dark period, I only tried to stay alive because of the teachings of the Catholic religion. We attended church assiduously; my mom was a catechism teacher every Sunday morning we'll all be in church. We regularly hammered the Ten Commandments. Above all, those who ended their own life would find themselves in hell. I therefore logically concluded that death by suicide was not admitted by God, and I didn't want to burn in hell. This fear of being burned for eternity was too strong, so I decided not to commit suicide.

At the age of twenty four years, while I was in an abusive relationship with the father of my children, I passed over a highway bridge and looked down at the cars passing at very high speed. Again, I thought about killing myself. I thought about getting crushed into little pieces by all these cars passing by. I thought it would be the end for me and all of my miseries. But once again, the vision of hell came to my rescue. I didn't want to burn for eternity, and so I stayed alive.

Yet my life felt like hell. At one point, I couldn't find the strength to go on living. I could no longer count on anyone. I didn't have anyone to count on; I didn't have anyone in my corner. The father of my kids made me believe that he was the only person who wanted me and really loved me. In other words, that was what he kept on telling me. He kept telling me that nobody loved me the way he did, and that he was the only person who thought of me and who wanted me. In fact, he was abusing me, manipulating me, and taking advantage of me. He did everything in his power to keep me away from everyone, even my own family, so that he could do whatever he wanted with me. He used to tell my mother, my sister, my brother-in-law, and my friends that I was crazy, that he treated me like a princess, and that I didn't know how to appreciate everything he did for me. In reality, he treated me horribly. He made everyone believe that I was the worst person that existed in the world and that he was the only person who was restoring my honour. He made my family and friends in Montréal scared of him. They did not want to be involved in helping me to get away from him. My own mother, sister, and brother in-law were on his side and treated me like I was less than nothing. I didn't know what to do. I didn't know how to get away from him or how to seek help. I felt very lonely and abandoned by all.

When I left my homeland Haïti to go to Montréal on April 15, 1990, I didn't know that I was going to learn how to survive. The person who picked me up at the airport kidnapped me and made me his concubine. He also considered forcing me to dance naked to get him money. Thanks to the help of a woman who had arrived shortly before me in Montréal, I was able to find my family and escape my oppressor.

While I was staying at my cousin's house with her family, I applied for refugee status. During my court hearing, one of the judges, a little chubby man with dark hair and a moustache gave me a superior look with disdain. He said that I did not look like a refugee and that my application was denied. I didn't know how a refugee was supposed to looks like.

When this happened, I had already met Claude. Claude had accompanied me to the hearing. When I came out, he looked at me and understood that my request had been refused. He told me that it was okay and we were going to get married so that I could become a Canadian citizen. This was the case, but at what price? Life with Claude was not rosy. Claude lived on welfare; he get $610 per month from the government. Because we got married, the amount was reduced to $310 per month. I was obligated to give him back the remaining balance every month. In addition, he had AIDS, but he did not bother to let me know about it until more than a year into the marriage. His doctor forced him to tell me. That's when I learned that he had carried the disease for more than six years already. I went to get tested, and my test results came back negative. Claude wasn't happy about it at all, like he wanted me to catch it. A couple years later, when Claude got too sick and was admitted into the hospital, his father learned that he was affected by the disease. Claude's father thought I was the person who had transmitted the disease to him. After Claude's death, the government looked for me to pay for his funeral. I didn't know I would live to tell my story.

Chapter 1

Montréal, May 29, 1990

Sadness and misery

The sadness and misery of this earthly life torment me. Why do you haunt me?

The sadness and misery of this shit life invade me day by day

Sadness, will you remember me in your dirty shit life?

Misery, God of our ancestors, you abandon me to my troubles

Sadness of my life, anything can happen to me in the blink of an eye. Who cares?

Don't bother

Misery, you promise that everything will work out one day. Will that day come soon?

Misery, God has put me to the test. I can't give up hope

Sadness, my God only knows why you give me this heavy burden to bear

Misery, tell me if I must bear this great burden with hope and courage

Misery, tell me that one day it will all be in the past, in the distant past

Sadness, promise me a smile will reappear on my lips by magic

Misery, my God won't let me down. I'm begging you; I need you in my life

Sadness, do you think God will eventually hear my prayers and my anguish?

Sadness, why do you hate me so much? Why do we hate each other that much?

My God, you command: "Love one another how I loved you." In my heart there will only be room for love.

I'm sad

I'm sad, I have problems that are just hardships
I'm sad, yet I don't despair 'cause I know God is there
I'm sad, but I know that God is omnipresent; he will support me and guide
me in my steps
I'm sad, but God will never let me down; he holds me firm. Here is my courage
I am sad, but I know that God is love and wisdom; he is everything to me
I'm sad, but I know God comes first in my life
My heart is filled with sadness now. What should I do?
Sometimes sadness weighs me down. The weight of this existence torments
me; life is killing me
The burden of this existence haunts me every day of my life; I'm sad
My loneliness becomes more and more my primary concern, but I do not
despair.

My adolescence, my life

My adolescence has passed in a cloud of dust; my life becomes sad
My life becomes more and more sad; my existence becomes more and more painful
My life becomes more and more lonely. No one loves me and yet I would like to be loved and love in return; I try to make friends, no one loves me
I would like to find love; unfortunately, no one loves me and this is a pity reality
It is really too bad. When I think about it, my life has no meaning, only disappointment and disappointment, one after the other one
Lord God, don't you think I'm worthy of loving? I have to face reality. I wonder if this is really my life. So lonely
Why do I always feel lonely? I thought I was loved, but that was just a dream
I was wrong; I keep wondering why I have this shitty life
Why am I so different? Why can't I live in harmony with myself?
Why are things so different for me? When will my life have meaning?
I try to be myself, to do the right thing, to only trust myself, to live for myself.

For your birthday

For your birthday, January 6, 1990, I wish you a happy birthday
For your birthday, I wish you much happiness and wealth
For your birthday, I hope that life is finally smiling at you and that you
are thinking of me
For your birthday, I hope your life will have meaning and you will think
about tomorrow
For your birthday, I hope you rejoice in your new loneliness
For your birthday, I hope your life is happy without me, and for always
On your birthday, I hope God speaks in your heart. Truly.

Chapter 2

May 12, 1990

Lord my God

Lord my God, forgive me for my iniquities; make me serve you with faith
and wisdom
Lord, my lovely God of mercy, make my life change; give me confidence
Lord my God, give me the courage to face the reality of this life
Lord my God, make me stronger than ever for what is coming my way
Lord my God, give me the strength to change what I can, to accept my fate
Lord my God, life so far from my home country takes another meaning
Lord my God, give me the strength to face my problems and my future
Lord my God, sometimes I wanna go back to my country forever
Lord my God, sometimes I think this is all just a bad dream.

Sometimes I think

Sometimes I think if I were home, if I were in my country, things would be different

Sometimes I think if I were home, a lot of things wouldn't have happened to me

Sometimes I think if I were home, the humiliation I experienced wouldn't have happened

Sometimes I think if I were home, all that I have faced wouldn't have happened

Sometimes I think if I were home, the leeches wouldn't mingle in my business

Sometimes I think I want to go back to my country; I consider the possibility

Sometimes I think I have to stay here because in my country life is not better

Sometimes I think my life is sad and has no meaning; down here, I face too many problems

Sometimes I think I've never had these issues before in my life

Problems that I was not used to. Me, who didn't understand anything at all

Me, who was so carefree, suddenly became worried, alone in this new life

Sometimes I think I have to be courageous and hopeful that one day it will all end well

God of my ancestors, I feel so sad, so far from my country, my family, my friends, from all that I know. I feel so far from my homeland who saw my birth.

My God

My God, look at me: I felt so good in my country; what have I become here?

My God, where did my life go? What can I do to get it back?

My God, I cry over my fate without being able to find a solution to my despair

My God, oh I want to go back to my country, to my dear homeland. There I felt good

My God, my life still had meaning. What am I doing here? I am not even legal

My God, I cried, I felt abandoned. I have no friends, no family. Here, I'm nothing

My God, help me, talk to me, tell me what to do, I implore you; have mercy on me

My God, my life is so sad in this new country; my love life no longer makes sense

My God, I don't know what it means to be loved by someone; I never learned

My God, I don't know what it means to count or to be important to someone

My God, I thought I was loved by my family, my friends, and the world around me

My God, I thought I was loved. I found out that I was never loved; my life made no sense

My God, I thought I loved him and he loved me too, but I was greatly mistaken

My God, I made the biggest mistake of my life. I was naive to think that you loved me

My God, I'm not ready to face reality; I'm not ashamed to say that I loved him

My God, I still love him. Finally, I miss everything: my life, my family, and my friends

My God, what does the future hold for me, me who was so carefree?

My God, sadness haunts me. Why are you tormenting me like this?

My God, why is happiness running away from me? I don't have the heart that deserves to be loved

My God, why am I not loved? My Lord God, I put my life in your hands

My God, do whatever you want with me. I am your child, after all. If you please, don't abandon me

Solitude

My loneliness weighs on me, my anguish bothers me, my sadness is adding to my setbacks

My loneliness makes me sick, so sick that I want to die, to leave this world

My loneliness is my eternal burden; I want to leave this cursed hopeless world

My loneliness is from a young age. My God, why don't you grant me my wish?

My loneliness reminds me of a child who seeks his mother's breast and can't find it

My loneliness, my God, I'm too young to face real life and fight this existence

My loneliness, as a child my life already weighed on me; I already felt all alone. My life is only the witness of my loneliness and misery

My God, why did you make me so that I'm always alone?

Lord, if you want me to always be alone, why don't you show me the way to follow?

Chapter 3

May 30, 1990

My existence

My existence, yet another me that goes away sadly and another one reappears

My existence and my life have no meaning. I am sad day after day because of my fucking life

My existence and my loneliness weigh on me; what should I do? My sentimental life is a fiasco

Lord God of my ancestors, will you accept me into your Kingdom? I will respect your will

Lord God of my ancestors, will you reject me? I will follow your path as long as you tell me what to do

Lord God of my ancestors, please make me want to live in this selfish life

Lord God of my ancestors, this bitch life haunts me from day to day; please don't let me down

Lord God of my ancestors, deliver me from my fornication, save my soul from all my sins, and make me better. Make my life meaningful.

My God, why?

My God, why my existence? Why can't I live in peace? Why I am not loved?
My God, my saviour, why doesn't love come to me the way I would wish?
My God, my master, why do I love and feel rejected in return? Why?
My God, I wish someone loved me more than I love him
I wish that he thought of me, that he gave me all his affection. I would love to live a perfect love life
My God, make the man I love think of me the same way that I think of him
My God, make me the centre of his thoughts so that he loves me and doesn't betray me
My God, why can't I be loved like everyone else? Why?
My God, why is my life so dumb? Sometimes I don't wanna be part of this world anymore if I have to live this life of misery, a life that is not mine.

My little plants

My little plants, how sad I am for you: you who smile, who bloom all year round

My little plants: you who sympathize with my pain, you who at least understand me

My little plants, my stalked life pities me, my mocked life makes me think about my loneliness

My little plants love; your beauty dazzles me every time I see you

My darling little plants, you don't ask for much, only that I take care of you

My little plants love; why do I feel torment to see you go?

My little plants, my life, why I feel so sad to see you wither and wither?

My little plants love; why do you leave me? Why is life so cruel?

My little plants love; even when you won't love me anymore, I won't and can never forget you

My little plants love; even if you leave me, I will love you for always

My darling little plants, come back to me. I'm ready to love you again as always; come back to me

My little plants love; my arms are wide open to receive you. Please come back

My little plants love; I hope that God speaks in your heart and that you see reality

May the sun shine on you. May your faces light up. Wake up one last time for me.

Sad life

My life is only sadness; my existence of a lonely dog tugs my innards
Sad life, without a look you go away, without a look you leave me, without a reason you're running away from me
Sad life, you're leaving. I'm here; I'm watching you go without being able to do anything
Sad life, what have I done to make you not love me anymore? What would I become without you?
Sad life, without your human warmth, without your sweet look like honey, you're leaving me
Sad life, your gaze melts my heart to pieces; you broke your promises
Sad life, what did you do with our memories? Was it just a dream?
Is this the life I deserve? The love you promised me, how sad.

However

However, I still loved you. I thought you loved me. What did you do with our memories?

Yet I loved you. What did you do with your promises? What happened to our love?

However, I thought we were happy together. It's just a distant memory

Yet my love life had no meaning before you; I didn't know how to live

However, before you I didn't know what true love was; I always believed that I was loved

However, I would like you to love me. I thought that with you everything was different. I'm sure I loved you and I thought you loved me too, but you went away; you left me with my sorrows, my loneliness, and my tribulations.

Chapter 4

June 1, 1990

Why don't you wanna love me?

Why don't you wanna love me and make me live the things that I never knew, why?

Why are you tormenting me? Though I loved you and I still love you; without you I feel alone

Why, without you, do I feel my life has no meaning? Without you I'm dead Everything is dead

Why don't you want me anymore? You made me feel confidence and now you are rejecting me

Why did you make me feel loved and then treat me in this inhuman way? Why?

I wonder why I was so naive to believe that you loved me. My life is empty without you

I hope that one day you will understand; I hope that one day you will experience what I have experienced. You lived what I lived and so you will know the suffering that you made me endure.

You leave me

You leave me without a look, without a smile, without remorse. All of a sudden there is no more room for me in your new life

You leave me without a word of regret; you felt for me only a look of disdain

You leave me without worrying about my future. I thought you loved me still, yet

you leave me without a word of pity. You have no more interest for me in your new life. How sad, really sad

You leave me today, your life is too busy, you have no more room for me in your heart

You leave me. I feel guilty that I cheated on you so stupidly without a reason

You leave me without a glance. Your lonely life doesn't want me anymore, yet I still love you

You leave me without knowing that despite everything I still love you; I want you in my life

You leave me. What happens to our beautiful memories together? They're already part of the past

You leave me without thinking about tomorrow, without thinking you too are human

You leave me without thinking that you can also make mistakes that I would understand

You leave me without a look, without a smile, so you have to quit us

You leave me. I guess you feel good and you don't want to build your life with me anymore

You leave me. You can't forgive me just once in your life. You have no heart

You leave me. What have you done with the words "I love you endlessly" that you used to whisper in my ears every day of our life together? You're selfish

You leave me. What have you done with our love? What have you done with our memories? Without me I hope your life will be warm and full of love.

Without a look

Without a glance, you go away. Without thinking, you leave me. Without a thought, our love is gone

Without a look, you leave me. I thought you loved me; I thought our love was eternal

Without a look, you run away from me. I'll never know why. What am I? What did I do to deserve this?

Without a glance, our life goes away. You are so cruel. Why are you leaving me like that? Why?

Without a look, you leave me for another one. Tell me, is she better than me?

Without a look, you don't love me anymore. I can't believe it. Without a word, you disappear from my life forever

Without a look, everything we stood for no longer exists, yet I thought we loved and understood each other

Without a glance, you leave me today. What does love mean for you? Nothing at all

Without a look, without a smile, you don't care anymore. What does a life of two represent for you?

I thought we were trying to get to know each other, to love each other wholeheartedly. What is that?

What is it for you? A game? It all ends as fast as it started; it's so sad.

With you

With you, I planned to make my life. I planned to love you until the end of my days
Why don't you want to understand me and love me as I am? I love you
Yet I think of you. I loved you wholeheartedly, yet I loved you and forgave myself
Why don't you want to love me anymore? It's a shame. Yet sincerely I loved you.

Tomorrow

Tomorrow, God willing, will be your birthday. I have nothing to offer you, only my sorrows

Tomorrow, God willing, will be your birthday, and my life is filled with complaints and fears

Tomorrow, God willing, will be your birthday. Your life will take another meaning; you're getting old

Tomorrow, God willing, will be your birthday. A new age will appear; your life is changing

Tomorrow, God willing, will be your birthday; new worries will be coming your way

Tomorrow, God willing, will be your birthday. Your life is in your hands. Do whatever you want with it: it's your call. You decide

Tomorrow, God willing, will be your birthday; it's up to you make good choices

Tomorrow, God willing, will be your birthday. Your life is in your hands; take good care of it

Tomorrow, God willing, will be your birthday. No one loves you more than yourself.

Chapter 5

June 2nd, 1990

My country

My country is screwed; my country has no future for the young people
My country has no more hope for me, only misery and sadness
My country has nothing to offer future generations; life is cruel
My country is fucked up. God of mercy, say something; do something
My country is cursed to the core. Why don't we have unison?
My country is devastated by the money and the greed of its people, people without education
My God, please do something for this cursed land.

God of my ancestors

God of my ancestors, why do you abandon us like this? Why are you abandoning us?

Are you giving up on us?

God of my ancestors, what fault, what crime, what evil have we committed to deserve this?

Merciful God, give us one more chance, one last chance, please

God of my ancestors, my country needs you. Have mercy on my people; I beg your pardon

My country, I would love to see you again. Nostalgia haunts me day by day in this new country

God of my ancestors, when will our tribulations end for a new day to come?

God of my ancestors, when can we be proud once again?

God of my ancestors, when can we hope for something from you?

God of my ancestors, when will you offer stability to your children in this country? When?

Today

Today, I am going to the Forum; I hope that God will provide me an answer to my fucking life
Today is a new day. I take courage and hope; trust I have in you
Today, I say thank you for everything; I beg you to say something, do something
Today, my heart is filled with happiness, yet I feel empty and sad
Today, anguish comes over me. I don't know what to do. Don't give up on me
Today, I would love to have happiness in my heart forever and think of nothing
Today, my life still has meaning and yet I feel so sad
Today, I wonder why I can't have a normal life
Today, I wonder again what I did wrong to deserve such a life
Today, finally, I told myself I love myself and nothing in the world will change that.

Sometimes

Sometimes I wonder what do I do with my life. Why do I exist? Why am I suffering?

Sometimes I wonder why can't I be happy. What is that? What did I do wrong?

Sometimes I wonder what have I done to the good Lord to deserve this shitty life

Sometimes I wonder why life torments me like this

Sometimes I wonder why, God, don't you take me? Do you not want me?

Sometimes I wonder why I can't finally live a life without history

Sometimes I wonder why do I live a life of endless nightmares

Sometimes I wonder why is my life so sad and seemingly next-day lacking

Sometimes I wonder why my ancestors don't help me. Why do they let me down?

Sometimes I wonder, fuck my life. What am I going to do with you?

Dirty shit life

Dirty shit life, when will you finally leave me alone? When?
Dirty shit life, when are you gonna let go of me? When?
Damn shit life, when will your rhythm stop? Fuck you, shit life
Dirty shit life, when are you gonna leave me alone?
Dirty shit life, go away. Leave me alone; finally, leave me alone
Dirty shit life, I want you to push yourself a little bit in my way
Dirty shit life, I want you to finally give me a chance to live
Dirty shit life, I want one last chance; that's all I'm asking of you.

Chapter 6

June 22, 1990

My life

My life, what have I done with you?
My life, what do you offer me?
My life, what harm have I done to you?
My life, what crime have I committed?
My life, what can I do if you don't give me a chance?
My life, my God, why can't I live a simple life?
My life, why can't you be so easy, just normal?
My life, why is the dollar race more important than humanity?
My life, oh the money, always the money, what becomes of you? You run the world
My life, why don't you stop tormenting me at last?

Nostalgic life

Nostalgic life, shitty life, what do you want from me?
Nostalgic life, life of misery, what are you doing with me?
Nostalgic life, life of sadness, life of joy, life of bluff
Nostalgic life, shitty life, what do you have in store for me?

What a life

What a shitty life! This life is not worth living
Why this life of sadness, tribulation, and loneliness?
Why this existence? Why is this life so difficult? I wonder why?
Why this shitty life? Why does this miserable life torment me like this?
Why is it always a struggle running after a life that doesn't want me?
Why am I fighting for a life that is not worth living?
Why does this existence hunt me like a chained dog? You piss me off.
Why do I feel stuck in a cage without being able to fly away?
Why this rot existence? Why?

Cruel life

Cruel life; sad, horrible, difficult life of despair and nightmares
Cruel life, especially far away from my country, my family, my friends, the familiar faces I know
Cruel life, I hate you. Why are you taking me away from everything I love?
Cruel life, what are you doing with me here in a foreign land, far away from all?
Cruel life, what would I become with you to remind me that I don't exist?
Cruel life, what are you finally doing with me? Would you let me down?
Cruel life, I couldn't believe you would let me down like this
Cruel life, talk to me, tell me, show me the way I must take
Cruel life, listen to me: take me out of the dead end that I'm in right now
Cruel life, look at me. Do you see my tears? I am in great pain.

Chapter 7

June 23, 1990

Help me

Help me, Lord God of my childhood; help me

Help me. You are my saviour, my master, my Father, so help me

Help me; don't let me down. I want to do your will; help me

Help me, support me, listen to me, talk to me, remember me, help me

Help me; I am ready to follow you wherever you want me to go

Help me; don't leave me in the wrong all my life

Help me, my God, on the path to success that I am pursuing

Help me, Lord God; you are the master of the universe. You can do whatever you want, so don't let me down. I'm begging you: help me.

How cruel you are

Life, how cruel you are! How sad you are!
Why this life? It does not mean anything
Why live, why suffer?
Why does this shitty life torment me like this?
My existence is so sad; my life is only sadness
My dog existence goes sadly; my life of misery haunts me
God of my ancestors, God of my existence, why this life?
Why do we have to suffer, to die? Life, why are you so cruel?
Why this life? Why must we suffer? Why be born if it's to be sad?
Why this existence if you always have to endure the worst?
Why this fucking life, why, why?

It seems to me

It seems to me that this life is not made for me; it only brings me despair
It seems to me that I was only born to suffer an eternal suffering
I was born in a country surrounded by suffering and misery
I would love to have a simple life, without ceremony, without worrying about tomorrow
I find myself facing all kinds of problems. My life is over; I get more lonely
My existence is sad; sometimes I think that God doesn't love me anymore, that He abandoned me
God, if you really exist, if you really love me and I'm your child, listen to my prayer
Listen to me, talk to me, tell me what I have to do, advise me, help me to get out of this impasse.

Rejection

This life doesn't want me. She mistreats me like a bitch; she kills me

My existence is like a trapped rat; she torments me day by day

My existence is making faces at me like a clown; my life is not worth living

This life doesn't want me; she takes away my honour, my family, my cheerfulness, my happiness, my hobbies, my studies, my friends; finally, she takes my everything away and leaves me with nothing

She leaves me all alone with my loneliness. My life is sad; God, have mercy and help me

Help me out of this mess that I find myself in. Help me, I am begging you

My life is in your hands; you're the only one who could still do something

Forgive me for my iniquities; forgive me for everything. I would like to serve you until the end of my life

You are my creator, my God. You represent everything; I belong only to you

Help me, please; don't let me fall like a sheet of paper. Please help me find my way

Help me to know who I really am. Help me; certainly don't let me down

Help me understand; you know my situation and I trust you.

Chapter 8

June 25, 1990

Lord God

Lord God of my ancestors, listen to my complaints, my moans, and my setbacks

Lord God of my ancestors, may your grace and kindness help me find the right way; please don't forget me in your Kingdom

Lord God, please accompany me in my efforts to success

Lord God of my ancestors, talk to me; tell me what to do. Do not abandon me. You will always be there to protect me, to lead me to the true path of life.

Sleep

I tried in vain to sleep but I can't; I feel a little funny. The lump in my throat remains my devoted companion. I feel she is trying to suffocate me at times. I have already taken two pills and I cannot fall asleep. My God, why this evil torments me like this? Say something.

The day I die

The day I die, don't cry on my grave
On the day of my death, on the contrary, laugh, sing, dance
When I'm dead, don't moan; have joy
When I'm dead, have no pain or regret
When I'm dead, remember me
When I'm dead, I'll protect you from up there
When I'm dead, I'll ask God to forgive you
When I'm dead, smile and think of the happiness that I brought in your life
When I'm dead, bring me red roses to remember my life
On the day of my death, I'll be happy in my last home
On the day of my death, I will be happy. I will not regret anything.

Is this that?

Do you sometimes think about this life and cry?
Do you sometimes think about this life and suddenly feel old?
Do you sometimes think about the life you have and think it could be better?
Do you sometimes ask yourself why this life? Why do you exist?
Do you sometimes ask yourself why do you live in this hypocritical world?
Do you sometimes ask yourself what is the meaning of your life?
Do you sometimes ask yourself why you are living this life?

Where has the love gone?

Where did the love you promised me go?
Where is he? What are you doing with me?
Where have your beautiful promises gone?
Where did the quiet life you promised me go?
You're just an animal, but at least the animals are thankful
You, on the contrary, are not; you are cruel
What are you? a bully
You will never be a real man
You will never have a real life
One day you'll have to stop
One day you'll have to ask yourself
What have I done with my life?
Why do I exist? Why did I exist?
Why doesn't life want me? You will reflect and think
What do I need to do to have a real life and good memories?
Beautiful, touching memories, beautiful enough for you to tell yourself with
a sigh that your life is full and that you have known happiness

Chapter 9

July 1, 1990

Pain

Why all the suffering in this shitty life? Why?
When can we have a chance to really live?
Can we really have it?
Life is so hard, sad, lonely, without mercy
Life is disturbing, heavy, exasperating
She's funny, unbearable, complicated
Why can't this life just be simple?
Why don't you say something, God?
Why don't you get involved?
Why are you letting us down?
We still trust you. Help us.

Nostalgia

Poor nostalgia, why are you coming to meddle in my life?
Nostalgia, why have I met you in my life?
Nostalgia, what have you done with my life, with my happiness?
Nostalgia, why do you tire me this way?
Nostalgia, what have I done to deserve you?
Nostalgia, nostalgia, will you go away and leave me alone?
Poor nostalgia, you're a bitch, you finally pissing me off, leave me alone.

Life

Life is really funny; why all these difficulties?
Why can't life be simple?
Lord God, please help me find the right way
Make things right at last. Is my life on the right track?
My life is so flat that in the end I wonder why I live
The nostalgia that I encounter every moment of my life makes me sick.

My last battle

My last battle: this will be the end; this will be my end
My last battle: this will be my annihilation
My last battle: this will be to rejoin my God
I will always fight for what I believe is right.

Chapter 10

July 10, 1990

My country

My nostalgia for my country, my parents, my friends, the Haitian people
My nostalgia makes me sick. I'm asking myself when will this end? When?
My God, say something. When will the tribulations end? When?
I'm asking myself and I will continue asking myself: when?
My God, do you hear my moans? Do you forget me? I can't believe it.

Fate, what are you doing with me?

Destiny, what are you doing with me? Where are you taking me?
Destiny, what would become of me without you? I only live for you
Destiny, what are you doing with me? I was only waiting for you
Destiny, what are you doing with me? Yet I met you yesterday
Destiny, what do you want from me? What do you have in store for me?
Destiny, your approach was wonderful. Why do you shame me?
Destiny, what do you have in store for me? Is it life, love, happiness, joy?
Destiny, will you tell me at last: have I found what I've been looking for?
Destiny, write to me. Tell me what to expect from you and what you want from me
Destiny, do I have to believe you? Will you abandon me?
Destiny, can I count on you to protect me?
Destiny, make me live. I cry to you out loud and at the same time very low
Destiny, don't forsake me. Support me; remember me
Destiny, love me, darling me. Caress me; make me lose my senses
Destiny, I love you already. I love you and I will love you forever
Destiny, I liked your approach, your intelligence intrigued me; don't make me ashamed
Destiny, I would like your warmth, your eyes, your lips, your body, your love, your weakness, your strength
Destiny, I would like you to give me your kindness forever; I want it all from you.

Love me

Why me? I loved you and you did not love me. Why?
God of my ancestors, tell me if the man you have reserved for me exists.
God of my ancestors, my life is just beginning. Tell me if it is already over.
God of my ancestors, tell me if love really exists.
God of my ancestors, is this the life I deserve?
God of my ancestors, my Father, my Master, finally tell me what you have in reserve for me.

Destiny

Destiny, finally make me live. I'm counting on you to finally bring me the
happiness that I dreamed of so much
Destiny, don't shame me; I need you to grow and live fully
Destiny, bring me the peace and warmth that I long-time longed for
Destiny, finally bring me the happiness that I never knew
Destiny, please don't leave me; stay with me for eternity
Destiny, don't leave me; love me.

My God, my Creator

My God, my Creator, show me the way to the truth
My God, my Creator, take my hand, lead me, choose for me
My God, my Creator, help me in my steps. Will you give me what I want?
My God, my Creator, will you give me a real home? I wish you loved me.
My God, my Creator, tell me what life has in store for me. What have you reserved for me?
My God, my Creator, I know you have the most wonderful things in the world in store for me
My God, my Creator, I would like the man you have reserved for me to really love me
My God, my Creator, I would like you to lead him to your Church
My God, my Creator, I know you do whatever you like, so please don't abandon me
My God, I don't wanna dream of a life I can't have. I need to know.

Chapter 11

September 1, 1990 at 1:20 a.m

He loves me, he doesn't love me

My God, make him love me really. I dreamed so much of a man like him
That he thinks of me, that he loves me as I am, not what I represent
May he love me with all my flaws and my qualities and give meaning to
my life
Make him really think of me; please, my God
I wish he really loved me; please give me this privilege
Help me find the love I have dreamed of since I was a child
Make him love me. Make it so that with him I find happiness
Make it an eternal happiness to which yourself consent.

In your arms

In your arms, I feel good; it's the assured dream
In your arms, I feel safe, invincible
In your arms, the world no longer exists
In your arms, I only have eyes for you
In your arms, my life takes its full meaning
In your arms, I'm happy
In your arms, you make me feel the joy of living
In your arms, my heart is filled with happiness
In your arms, I completely forget myself
Is that for a moment or for life?
I would like to know. I would like to not be disappointed.

I love you already

I love you already, strong enough to be able to tolerate you
I love you already, enough to finally be able to say that I found what I was
looking for
I love you already, enough to say that I met the man of my life
I love you already, so I'm able to rest in your arms
I love you already, so I'm able to feel myself loved by you
I love you already, enough to say that you are my destiny
I love you already, so I can scream it out loud
But if you leave me, this will be the end for me
I always asked God to give me an ideal husband
I don't know yet what you are to me
But I would like you to be the husband that God has reserved for me
Don't give up on me; stay with me
Your eyes tell me that you think of me
Your eyes tell me that you love me
I hope I'm not mistaken; it would be too hard.

Your blue eyes

Your blue eyes tinted with green tell me that you think of me
Your blue eyes tinged with green tell me that you love me; is that true?
Your blue eyes tinted with green make me forget who I am
Your blue eyes tinged with green tell me you're mature
I love your greying hair; it tells me that you've lived
It tells me that you have experience
Your greying hair reminds me of fate
A destiny that I forged for myself, without ulterior motive, head down
I would not like to be disappointed, because I love you already
I got attached to you wholeheartedly
Your greying hair reminds me of so many things
If only you knew how I feel about you.

Chapter 12

Now

Now my life is in your hands; take good care of it
Now make me a woman; give me the love I so longed for
Now make me a woman and be my Master
Now make me a woman so that I can become your mistress
Now make me a woman so that our paths meet
Now make me a woman for you, only for you; teach me about life
Now make me a woman you pamper day after day
Now make me a woman by your side year after year
Now make me a woman you will never forget.

Love of my life

Love of my life, will I finally find you?
Love of my life, tell me if you will make me happy
Love of my life, please don't shame me
Love of my life, listen to me and do me a big favour
Love of my life, make it true; make me not disappointed.

September 3, 1990 at 11 p.m.

A new love

A new love begins; it's a new beginning
New life dawns; make it real
My God, my creator, my universe, make it real
I would so much like to believe in you
I wish I could trust you so much
My desire is for us to be together forever
I love you already; I already think about you
It's like we've known each other forever
I dreamed so much of your understanding, your friendship, and your love
My God, make it true.

Love

Love of my life, will I finally find you?
Tell me, will you make me happy forever?
Tell me you'll stand by my side and you won't shame me
Listen to my lamentations and don't disappoint me
My Almighty God, make it true.

My God, why?

Why does this only happen to me?
Why can't I be really happy?
Why can't I be loved like everyone else?
Why, my God, does life bother me like this? Why?
Why are you mistreating me in this shit life? Why?
Why, shitty life, don't you leave me alone?

Chapter 13

September 4th, 1990

Life of misery

Life of misery, life of hunted dog, when will you leave me in peace?
Life of misery, when will you finally leave me alone?
Life of misery, why can't I be happy like everyone else?
Life of misery, tell me, because I would like to know, am I only made to suffer?
Life of misery, how sad you are. My existence is cruel
Life of misery, you pity me; you pity me
Life of misery, was I born of the latter rain?
Life of misery, why can't my life be stable?
Life of misery, why do I always have to suffer? Why?
Life of misery, why does life torment me so?
Life of misery, go away, leave me alone.

Leave me

Leave me alone, dirty shit life. Go away, go away, leave me in peace
Leave me alone, finally give me my life, go away, go away
Leave me alone; go with all your misery
Leave me alone; go with all your worries
Leave me alone; don't forget to fuck yourself
Leave me alone; finally, leave me alone.

André

André, my little André, my little blanc-bec, are you thinking of me?
André, my little André, do you think I love you?
André, my little André, well, you're wrong
André, my little André, if that's what you think
I don't wanna see you again; don't call me anymore
Good riddance for all; if I am not accepted, I can always go back home
At least I still have a home; thank you, my God
With a heavy heart, I'll say go fuck yourself and also tell myself this is life

Positive - Negative

Positive: life is a gift; that would be good
Negative: it won't be the end of the world
My little white angel, do you think I give myself to you like this?
Do you think I'm desperate to stoop down in front of you for your fucking city?
Well, you're wrong. You'll make a big mistake; you'll regret it
I want a life not like this; I want to live a carefree life not like that
I want a life that I can finally call happiness; I can finally say that I am living.

Love each other

Love is for life, not for a moment
To love is to feel loved in return
Love is mutual respect
To love is to take care of each other
To love is to be faithful to each other
To love is to want each other
To love is to say goodbye to pleasure without the other one
To love is to get used to each other
If there is no more love between us, why be together?
If there is no more love between us, why waste time?
If there is no more love between us, why say I love you over and over?
If there is no more love, why end up getting married?

Chapter 14

My little love

My little white love with blue eyes tinted green
My little white love with slippery greying hair
My little white love, I'm already getting used to you
My little white love, I already love you
My little white love, I'm already thinking of you
My little white love, why are you asking me if I love you?
My little white love, you know that love comes without notification
My little white love, why so many questions?

Do you think

Do you think I want to have fun with you?
Do you think I'm lying when I say I love you?
Do you think I'm wrong, that I'm crazy?
Do you think I'm not thinking of you?
Do you think that I don't really love you?
Do you think I love you for something?
Do you think I am complicated?
Do you think my life is lonely and that I need you?
Do you think you give me hope and courage to continue living?
Do you think we were meant to be together for life? Do you, do you think?

Why do you ask me if I love you?

Why do you ask me if I love you? Why finally?
Why do you ask me how much I love you?
Why are you complicating things?
Why don't you want to understand?
I would have loved to cry out loud that I love you
I wish you had trusted me
I wish you would love me like I love you
I would have loved to tell you how many plans I have for our life together
I would have loved to tell you that with you I feel complete; without you
I am lost
I wish I could tell you don't give up on me; I love you
I just wish I could tell you that I want to live by your side forever.

Your eyes

Your eyes, your tender eyes make me forget the time
Your eyes make me lose my mind without reserve
Your eyes make me forget my desire for adventure
Your eyes make me forget myself
Your blue eyes tinted with green make me see the ocean
Your eyes take me around the world
Your eyes are so beautiful they look like a rare flower
Your eyes make me want to live for eternity
Your eyes look like the love you are giving me
Your eyes look at me and in them I get lost
Your eyes make me feel the desire you have for me
Your eyes I can see myself inside
Through your eyes, my life is in your hands.

I get lost in you

I get lost in you; I would love to tell you "love me"
I get lost in you. Take me; do whatever you want with me
I lost myself in you; I belong to you for eternity
I lost myself in you; my body and my heart are yours
I lost myself in you; everything in me claims your attention and desires you
I lost myself in you; I hope you love me and to love you until the end.

Chapter 15

your hair

Your hair, your greying hair is beautiful and shining like crystal
Your greying hair reminds me of the happiness you bring me
Your greying hair I love and admire day after day
Your greying hair releases a jasmine scent to my nose
Your greying hair, oh I love running my fingers on them
Your greying hair, how I love to feel them touching my skin
Your greying hair, I wanted to say how much I love them
Your greying hair that I love so much; Oh! how cute they are.

My God

My God, my Creator, make him really love me
My God, my Creator, make it true
My God, my Creator, make him think of me
My God, my Creator, make him represent my universe
My God, my Creator, what do you have in store for us?

September 6, 1990 at 10:15 p.m.

Why?

Why don't you call me? Don't you think about me?
Why am I calling and you don't answer? Have you already forgotten me?
Why don't you talk to me? Why don't you pick up your phone?
Why are you keeping silent? Aren't you tempted to see me anymore?
Why are you keeping your distance? Am I boring you already?
Why? I wonder what I did to you?
Why my God, does he despise me like this?
Why? I feel so alone and devastated. Why? Tell me; I am begging you
Why don't you answer me? Call me; talk to me please.

Friendship

Before, you didn't have any interest in me, and now you telling me that you are my friend

Now you keep telling me that you are my friend forever. Why now? Tell me, what has changed?

Now, you are telling me that you are giving me your unlimited friendship. Why?

Remember that I am very happy to accept this friendship; but why now?

Now you are telling me that you are my friend and yet you are avoiding me; why? Why are you so hesitant?

Now you are telling me that you are my friend; why are you so afraid of me?

Why are you walking away from me now? Is it because of my status?

Does my status cause you so much pity? Is that why you are hiding from me when you see me coming?

I would love your friendship more than anything else in the world, unfortunately

Now you are running away from me. I would love to be proud of your friendship, but at what price are you giving it to me?

Honestly, I would love to know why you want to be my friend, please

Sincerely, I accept your friendship with all my heart, and without reservation, but I don't want your pity, ever

If it's because of my situation, I sincerely don't want your shitty pity

Honestly, you can keep your dirty friendship; I don't want it. I do not want nothing by your pity

For me, sincere friendship is worth more than money and love. You are scaring me with your hypocrite friendship

Chapter 16

Finally

Finally, in the end, animals really are best friends; at least they are faithful
They love you wholeheartedly, they are sincere, they love you until the end of time
You, you are just a man, a man with desires, like all other men who exist
Why do you tell me that you are my friend when it is not true? When it is a lie
Your friendship I won't need. Don't worry; I will survive. After all, I'm not still on the verge of despair.

My life

My life is hard, my life is sad; what have you done with me?
Why do you torment me like this? Why do you treat me this way?
Why don't you leave me in peace? What will become of me? What do you have in store for me?
Why a life of misery and loneliness? Why? Why this life of a stalked dog? Why?
Why the hell are you bothering me like this? What have I done to you?
What do you want from me? Will you leave me alone one day?
Go away; leave me alone already. Leave me alone with my suffering
Why does my pain, my loneliness, concern you so much? Leave me alone
Go away. Go away and don't bother to come back anymore. Go away with all your miseries
Let me live, let me go, and make sure you don't come back.

You

You: a smile, a look, a gesture, and I already think of you
You: a nice little word. You are already part of my life; you got my attention
You: with your eloquent approach, you flood my life with immense happiness
What do you mean to me: happiness, love, or pain?
You: are you my life, or my misfortune? Please tell me: who are you?
You: what do you represent for me? Suffering or infinite happiness?
You: with your blue eyes tinted with green, you remind me of the blue sky
You: with your blue eyes tinted with green, you flood my heart with sparks
You: with your blue eyes tinted with green, you fill me with infinite happiness
You: with your greying hair, you remind me of the father that I never had
You: with your greying hair, you make me forget that time exists
You: with your greying hair, I want you to love me
You, with your greying hair, caress me until the end of time
You, with your greying hair, make love to me like it is the first time
You make love to me like a bully; don't stop
You make me forget that the world exists; please love me
Hey you, don't let me down. Love me; give me confidence
Hey you, make me understand life exists. How could I forget you?
Hey you, you give me courage in this cursed world
Hey you, do you know that since my childhood my life is only sadness?
Hey you, I'm in bitter pain; I need you in my life.

Memory

Memory of my life, what are you doing to me? What do you reserve for me?
Memory, you are already only memory. Hey you, you are already my past
Memory, my hopes are gone to shreds; my thirst for love is dried up
Remember, you are already part of my past
Remember, your only desire is to make love to me
Remember, you go away with your complications; I don't regret you
Remember, I don't regret anything. Life goes on
Remember, I go my way; I keep on living
Remember, I say to God, "no hard feelings," none ...

Chapter 17

I'm tired of you

I'm tired of you. Why all these complications?
I'm tired of you. Why be born, grow, live, and finally die?
I'm tired of you. Why leave all these beautiful things?
I'm tired of you. What do you represent for me?
I'm tired of you. I wonder why every day.
My life, I'm tired of you. I'll never stop wondering why.

My God of my ancestors

God of my ancestors, you alone have the key to the mystery of life
God of my ancestors, protect me, help me, please don't let me down
God of my ancestors, despite all my nonsense, forgive me
God of my ancestors, is this is my destiny?
God of my ancestors, I beg you to grant me your forgiveness
God of my ancestors, I know I don't deserve you; I don't deserve your love
God of my ancestors, give me your grace; please give me one more chance.

Nostalgia, my nostalgia

Nostalgia, my nostalgia, I think of you once again; what became of you?

Nostalgia, my nostalgia, I think of you all the time; I think about all the beautiful things we could do together

Nostalgia, my nostalgia, where are you now? What are you doing now? What are you becoming?

Nostalgia, my poor nostalgia, what future do you have now? Do you think about me?

Nostalgia, my poor nostalgia, where are you going? Wait, don't go yet. What's your hope for me?

Sweet love

Sweet love that comes to haunt my dreams
Sweet love, would you like me to be yours for life?
Sweet love, would you love me just to have a moment in my arms?
Sweet love, drunkenness of my fucking life, will you shame me?
Sweet love, would you leave me in the moment that I need you the most?
Sweet love, the song of my heart hums so that my life has meaning
Sweet love, my desire is for someone to love me the way I am
Sweet love, immense ocean which tenderly floods my heart with its gentle wave
Sweet love, will you come back to make me relive unforgettable moments?
Sweet love, I only think of you with my little heart
Sweet love, I would love to hear your tender voice once again
Sweet love, tenderly, take me to the land of no time
Sweet love, together would we come to fly high?
Sweet love, emerge from my endless dream. Would I hear the phrase "I love you"?
Sweet love, will I ever hear the words "I love you; I will never forget you"?

Chapter 18

October 10, 1990

Midnight

Midnight, I can't stop thinking about you, so I am writing to you
Midnight, I can't stop thinking about you, so I am calling you
Midnight, I can't stop thinking about you; you are my life
Midnight, I can't stop thinking about you; you are my love
Midnight, I can't stop thinking of you at the time of our most beautiful love story
Midnight, I can't stop thinking about you; your image haunts me in an unconditional way
Midnight, I can't stop thinking about you; I wonder what you are doing now
Midnight, I can't stop thinking about you; do you still think about me?
Midnight, I can't stop thinking about you; do you remember me in your kingdom?
Midnight, I can't stop thinking about you; does your heart beat when you hear my voice?
Midnight, I can't stop thinking about you; my life is yours if you want it
Midnight, I can't stop thinking about you; what will you do with me?

Do you remember?

Do you remember the fourteenth of September; it's already been almost a month?

Do you remember it has been almost a month since I said "yes" to you?

Do you remember I said yes to your love and it was wonderful?

Do you remember it was the most important day of our fucking lives?

Do you remember that I hope our love will last until the end of our life?

Do you remember it was so magical that our life had finally taken one direction?

Do you remember that by your side I felt good? Do you remember we felt good together, and I wouldn't want to go anywhere else?

Do you remember that by your side I felt loved and safe in your arms?

Do you remember I thought to myself that I had finally found the man of my dreams?

Do you remember when I whispered in your ears, "I love you infinitely"?

Alone in my corner

Alone in my corner, I think of you
Alone in my corner, I wonder what are you doing now?
Alone in my corner, I need you; where are you?
Alone in my corner, what do you do with my love for you?
Alone in my corner, do you still think of me? Do you really love me?
Alone in my corner, I wonder if you really love me like you say
Alone in my corner, I wonder if these are second-hand words or forever
Alone in my corner, I wonder if these are words without any importance
Alone in my fucking corner, I am thinking of my childhood
Alone in my fucking corner, who can I finally count on?
Alone in my fucking corner, God of my ancestors, I implore your great mercy
Alone in my fucking life, God of light, help me; don't leave me to fall
Alone in my fucking life, God of my ancestors, protect me; guide me toward your house
Alone in my fucking life, my future is in your hands; you alone know my future
Alone in my fucking life, you are the God of Gods, the God of mercy, omnipresent Powerful God, I need your presence now. Please help me: I trust you to set me free of my chains.

Live your life

Live your life; don't tell me you love me when you treat me like shit
Live your life and leave me alone; let me live mine
Live your life; for me, you don't matter anymore. Go play elsewhere
Live your life; you are just a child. Why did you lie to me without any valid reason?
Why, why did you invite me to the movies and not keep your promise?
Why? I didn't ask you to invite me; I was fine without you
You are still a child; you don't have any respect or personality
Why did you tell me you would come to see me? You never came. You know you didn't have to
Why did you lie to me so brazenly? Why? Why?
Yet you were so nice, so different. Why did you lie to me? It didn't make no sense
Why? Does it bring you glory? Why?

I'm fed up

I'm fed up with my life, this life of misery that you gave me
I want to end my life. What can I expect from you?
I love you. I didn't dare admit it to you for fear that you would laugh at me
I was scared to show that I fell in love with a child
I was afraid of what you might think if I told you. I was afraid you would take me for a fool and laugh at me
I was afraid of failure. What do you have for me, you, my new love?
I wonder if you really love me like you told me
I wonder, are you thinking about me right now? What will become of my life?
My God, my Creator, please say something.

Chapter 19

I think of you

I think about you, but with all my heart I tell you fuck you

I think about you, but you betrayed me. With all my heart, I still tell you fuck you

I think about you, but you never loved me. I still tell you that you are a piece of shit

I think about you, but who are you? I won't stop telling you fuck you

I think about you, but who do you think you are treating me like this? I don't care about you anymore

I think about you, but why did you lie to me so bitterly? I hate you now even more

I think about you, but it has to come to this. I'll never trust you again

I think of you, but I tell you with all my heart, once again, fuck you.

I love you

I love you; I don't wanna waste your life because you have a lot to learn
I love you, but you are just a child and your life has just started
I love you, but my life is over. I have no hope left
I love you, but I feel old, too old for my age
It's shame to say that I am only twenty-one years old, would you believe me?
My life, my fucking life, what did I do to deserve you?
What would it become? Oh my God! Send me your peace
Send me the love you have reserved for me. The perfect love

I was born

I was born in a country filled with problems, miseries
I was born in a world filled with differences, wickedness, suffering
I was born in a world filled with selfishness, prejudice, and hypocrites, without the fear of God, without faith or law
I was born in a world in which my passage through this cursed land meant nothing
I was born in a world that I do not understand; I wonder what I am doing here?
I was born in a world that makes me want to go back where I come from
I was born in a world that is so turned upside down that I want to have my peace far away from everything
My God, take me with you. Take me from this damn life; I am imploring your mercy.

Solitude

Solitude: I lived a life of solitude, the life of a stray dog, a life that doesn't want to leave me alone

Solitude, I lived a hopeless life. My God, tell me I was born just for that

Solitude, do you remember me? Do you remember your promise of peace? Why can't I be like everyone else?

Loneliness, do you remember you promised to make me a happy life? Why am I so alone?

Loneliness, I think about my life without a father figure to cuddle me, to love me, to protect me

Loneliness, I think about my childhood life without a mother who loves me, who protects me, who fights for me.

A mother who has already suffered, a mother who already carries the weight of life, a mother without a mother and a father to protect her as a child

Loneliness, I think of my life without love, with a mother who never shows me love that she never had herself, with a mother who couldn't protect herself, with a mother who couldn't give me all I desire, with a mother who fights to survive, with a mother who gives me her love in her own way. I feel like a stranger in my own country with a family that doesn't want me. I have always been alone since my childhood of misery, yet I would like someone to love me, someone to show me that I am important, that I am worthy. I would like to trust someone, but I can't.

Meet

I met you on August fourth; I thought you were romantic

I thought it was too sudden, yet it seems that you are sentimental

I didn't know until Sunday, November fourth, when you showed me your true nature

I hoped that you would have some nice surprises in store for me and I would be very happy; I was wrong

I hoped to have my last experience with you. My life would have been full of happiness

Still, I hoped I wasn't wrong. It would be too hard, really hard, to think of an end

I was starting to get used to your sweet voice so charming that I wanted to hear it forever

I was starting to feel like I couldn't be without you for a second

I kept thinking of you as someone dear to me. Will you meet my expectations?

I would like to know if you will rethink my desires. Can I count on you forever?

Can you love me like I deserve? Can I trust you with my whole heart?

Can I give you my heart forever? And will you love me back in return the way that I love you?

Can you meet all my expectations? I wish it with all my heart.

Chapter 20

February 1, 1991 at 11:45 p.m.

Cry

Cry, cry, what's the use of crying? What do tears bring me?
Cry, cry, crocodile tears bring nothing but tears of discouragement
Cry, cry, to express the resentments of my bitch life
Cry, cry, what good are tears? What are you meddling with? Life is life
Cry, cry, what's the point of tears? It's really no use
Cry, cry, what's the point of tears? They don't bring you the life you have lost
Cry, cry, what good are tears? They only bring a deep despair
Cry, cry, what good are the crocodile tears that you shed without any remorse?
Cry, cry, what good are tears of pity? Nobody cares about you.

Live

Live, live, what's the point of living without knowing if tomorrow we'll still be here?
Live, live, what's the point of living if we don't have love, if there's no one who loves us?
Live, live, what's the point of surviving if you have no one to rely on in life?
Live, live, why life? Why existence? This way of life is killing me
Live, live, why do you torment me like this? Why this shitty life?
Live, live, why don't you leave me alone at last?

My God, why?

My God, why is everything against me? Is this my fate?
My God, why live in this cursed and hopeless world?
My God, why, Lord, don't you take my life away? Why?
My God, why do I live? In what honour?
My God, why don't I even deserve your grace?
My God, why does everyone want to order me around? Why?
My God, I'm sick of everything, sick of all this shitty life
My God, why am I begging for my existence in such a hypocritical world?
My God, why do I live in a world without mercy, without faith or law?
My God, why don't you take my life away? Please take me with you this very evening; I have suffered too much.

Mother

Mother, mother, do you see what misery I endure in this crazy world?

Mother, did you think of me when you gave birth to me? Did you think of my future?

Mother, you knew how to raise me but you didn't teach me happiness

Mother, you didn't teach me not to trust; you didn't give me the importance that I deserve

Mother, you didn't teach me about real life, to beware of liars and manipulators

Mother, do you see what I'm going through here, far away from you, far away from my homeland, far away from everything and everyone I know?

Mother, mother, help me. Can I still fight in this thankless life of hypocrites and the merciless?

Mother, do you see what suffering I am enduring? I will never know real happiness

Mother, I have been in pain since birth. I have known horror from the day I was born

Mother, why did you bring me into this world, into this cursed and selfish world?

Mother, mother, can you see what I am going through and understand me?

Mother, you never understood me. Will you be able to when I am dead?

Mother, tell me something: does my life have meaning? What a sad waste

Mother, my life of misery, of bamboo, doesn't make no sense. I am rotten by the system of this cursed world

Mother, do you see what I am going through in my life today? If you had taught me love, if you had taught me to love myself, I would have known how to defend myself and protect myself from the evil of this world

Mother, I would have known why I live and why I am here in this world today. I could have a better life.

Mother, why did you put me in this evil world? Did you think of me?

Mother, did you think about all of this?

Mother, did you think you were doing a good deed? Yet where I was, I felt good

Mother, mother, why did you put me in this cursed world, this world of hopeless selfishness? Why?

My lonely life

My lonely life, stray bitch, am I doomed to live on my own?
My lonely life, why do I feel all alone in my fucking life?
My lonely life, I ask you why others have so much happiness and not me
My lonely life, why my life? Why was I born in this cursed country?
My lonely life, why am I here below? What fault, what crime, have I committed?
My lonely life, I ask your forgiveness. Lord, forgive me for my iniquities
My lonely life, accept me into your world; support me on your shoulder
Let me finally find comfort.

Chapter 21

The day of my death

The day of my death, when will you finally arrive?
The day of my death, when will I finally get my peace?
The day of my death, when will I finally meet you?
The day of my death, I wish you would come now and then I could say farewell to my friends, farewell to you, farewell to my family, farewell to everyone
Farewell to those I know, to those I have known, and to those I will never know, farewell
Goodbye to this rotten world, goodbye to misery, goodbye to myself, goodbye.......

You

You who said you loved me, tell me if it was the truth
You who said we were made to live together, were you lying to me?
You who said you couldn't live without me, was that true?
You, yes you, were you really real? Did you really think so? Why?
Today, on a whim, with a stroke of madness, you decided to leave me
You told me we were not made to live together, yet what has changed?
You, with all the problems that you brought to me, I thought it was a normal life
You, who told me that the problems we face are part of the love we feel
You, did you really understand me? Did you make the effort to understand me, to respect me?
You, if you had at least made an effort, we wouldn't have come to this
You, before you were nothing, now you think that you represent something
Today you decided to reject me. Who do you think you are?

Before

Before you were nice, sweet; was it to lure me into your trap?

Before you were nice, sweet; what happened to you? You changed; why?

Before you were nice, sweet; now you are going wild. Tell me why?

Before you were nice, sweet; I can't believe you have changed. After all, you are just a man

Before you were nice, sweet; I am starting to regret doing anything with you

Before you were nice, sweet; maybe for once I should listen to my instinct

Before you were nice, sweet; I never should have thought to live with you and

let you treat me the way you have treated me

Before you were nice, sweet; now mean that you are, is God in your heart?

Before you were nice, sweet; did you want us not to be together anymore? I didn't think so

Before you were kind, sweet; my God, my Creator, tell me, is it coming from you?

Before you were nice, sweet; I accepted you as you were, with nothing, and yet I loved you

Before I loved you, I thought we would end up spending our entire lives together.

Such a waste

What a waste, naive that I was, after all, you're just a man
A selfish, conceited, shameless man who thinks only of one thing: yourself
Where are you leading me? Where are you going in this world? I cannot believe it
I can't hold you back forever; you have a choice to go away and forget about me
But my life is empty without you. What could I do without you?
When can I free myself from the sorrow you brought to me?
I thought you loved me; I thought our choice was final
Maybe I exaggerated, but that doesn't mean I didn't love you
That doesn't mean I didn't think of making you happy every day of our lives
More than anything else, I would like to know what to do. You're leaving me
That's life, we can't change it, now go away; I won't hold you back
By your acquired arrogance, by your selfishness, you decide to leave me, so be it
Did you make the right choice? I'm happy for you; that's what you want
I'm leaving. I hope you made the right choice and that you will be happy for eternity.

Your choice

I hope you made the right choice in life
I know you will never find a woman like me
I forgot myself; I devoted myself to you and loved you despite everything
I loved you; I thought you loved me too. You were nothing; you had nothing
Without me you are nothing; without me you will ever be nothing, yes,
without me you are nothing
You will become nothing again, like you were when I picked you up, nothing
Now you feel like a big boy to leave me; that's my reward
After all that I've done for you, all that I've sacrificed for you
I have to accept it and go away, and you keep everything
But does your heart approve of the decision you've made?
Why haven't you thought of the two of us, selfish that you are?

Chapter 22

April 27, 1995 at 4 a.m.

Already

Already, when I was 20 years old, I felt like a 90-year-old, and now
Now I'm 25 years old, I feel even older; the years have passed so quickly
Already the years have left their mark. Oh youth, mad youth, what have you made of me?
Already the water has flowed under the bridges. My life is only a mystery; it's unfair
Already misery still haunts my days; what have I done to deserve you?
I have already asked the great God to come to my aid, but it seems to me, it seems He hasn't heard me
Already I wonder when my prayers will be answered

Itinerant

My house is my coat; I ask for a penny here and there to live
My stomach is hollow; I'm starving; I sleep in the street, in the subway
I sleep anywhere. Friends, I have plenty of them in good times
My heating is a manhole cover, overrun with rats
My house is my coat, a barely lined three-quarters
I'm cold to the bone; it's winter, after all
Yet I'm the happiest person in the world
I have already known the poverty of wealth
The only advice I give you is to be satisfied with the little you have
And you will be happy. My house is my coat, a three-quarter double
I am the richest person in the world.

The day we met

The day we met, in the summer of 1992, I wish never existed
The day we met I would have cursed forever, if only I had known
The day we met, my life changed forever; you changed it for the worse
The day we met I would like to erase forever from the history of my life
The day we met, I made the mistake of being too nice and letting you approach me
The day we met, I made the mistake of letting you sit by my side
The day we met, I wish I had detected the wickedness that lives in your heart
The day we met, I wish I would have known the tribulations that you would bring to me in this shitty life and run far away from you forever.

Author
Judith Juste

www.ingramcontent.com/pod-product-compliance
Lightning Source LLC
Chambersburg PA
CBHW031313060726
47590CB00003B/1194